Vision

Perspectives from a vital lens

Precious Eda

ISBN 978-93-5559-228-6

Published in India 2022 by Pencil

A brand of
One Point Six Technologies Pvt. Ltd.
123, Building J2, Shram Seva Premises,
Wadala Truck Terminal, Wadala (E)
Mumbai 400037, Maharashtra, INDIA
E connect@thepencilapp.com
W www.thepencilapp.com

With over 15 years spent in leading young people at various levels, he lives with a commitment towards growing more leaders through teaching leadership and personal development.

A Speaker, Teacher, Mentor to many and a trained Attorney.

His #iLeadership brand is a flagship hashtag that floods out tons of blogs, tweets, videos and posts on leadership and personal development.

*** This work is specifically designed to help leaders facing challenges in working with their top leaders and bosses as they strive to make positive impacts on their organisations and groups.

*** With a commitment to making leadership principles less complicated and easy to transfer, Precious Eda has dedicated a series of mini-books that deal with specific areas of leadership in a bid to making them easy to understand and apply to everyday situations. Other sub-topics covered in his series of mini-books include: Vision, Values, and Teamwork.

*** Precious Eda is blessed to share his life with Amarachi Loveth his amazing wife.

CONTENTS

First - What's with vision 16

Second - Why do we need vision 19

Third - What can we take away from all that 24

Fourth - How do we get our vision 28

Fifth - What's next after knowing the vision 33

Sixth - Your vision and you 38

Seventh - Is the vision different from the mission 41

Eighth - What's to be done after all's been said 43

Cool quotes on vision!! 46

Preface

As a young leader and being involved in youth leadership and campaigns at various levels, I've noticed a few challenges with young people especially with regards to personal development and taking effective actions to achieve self and group growth and success. Many young leaders read books, many attend lots of seminars and download a lot of podcasts and mp3s, and in fact there is a lot of material in the market and on the internet available to everyone. But when you compare the quality of materials available to the quality of leadership we have in our society, they are amazingly not in consonance. I have burdened my thoughts with this issue for quite a while and just had to think up a solution. The questions to be solved hover around, why are our young people failing in their lives? Why are our problems with leadership becoming worse rather than improving even with all the information we have? What quality of leadership do we have and what kind of leaders are we breeding for the future?

Well I may not have the final answers to the puzzle, because I believe that we have come to the times where as a generation, for us, many things can only get worse. But that doesn't mean we would resign to fate and just pose mute while the world shuffles into calamity. I mean, where would my children fulfil their own dreams if our world goes into uncontrollable crazy? So for this cause I had to ask myself, what could be done to help young people and leaders in my nation and around the world to become better and more effective in changing the lives of their people and themselves and adding values to the lives around them? There are two things I believe are lacking in the transfer of quality leadership from one generation to another; effective mentoring and commensurate action. With the advancement in technology and everybody on earth shifting their "sphere of influence satellite stations" to the social media and all the other 21st century communication platforms, it is quite easy to achieve the two lacking items.

Leaders who believe that their calling is to serve their people and touch the lives of people in many positive manners must wake up to the reality of being more intentional and effective about mentoring and seriously supporting more of their people in reaching success in leadership at various levels of influence.

I understand that a good number of great leaders are already doing this in tremendous patterns, I am a beneficiary of some of such intentional mentoring programs and so I understand how important it is for more leaders to start replicating what they learn and acting what they teach. To be able to effectively pursue this course of transferring quality leadership, leaders must be able to submit to more learning and be willing to receive more followers. This way, the more you learn is the more you teach. And if everyone tries to do this, we will have a duplication of real quality. Individuals will improve, families will grow and nations will transform. The One Point Series aims to take leadership issues one point at a time and deal with them in really simple ways and suggest simple effective action points for the reader.

The series gives the reader at a glance the very solution to a leadership puzzle without too much illustration. It serves as an easy access manual for easy reference and it is easy to read and digest and even memorise. With not so many pages, leaders can easily study an issue and with the simple lessons learnt try to develop other leaders. Leaders also have access to various platforms upon which they can connect with me and we can share our ideas and experiences and questions on each of the issues on any point in the series.

The goal of the series is to share my thoughts and experiences on leadership and personal development issues with as many leaders as possible and create an opportunity for as many leaders and people as possible to get better from learning from me and for me to grow faster by learning from them too.

As I always say, my purpose in life is to make sure that people become better than they were before they met me after they meet me.

So, enjoy the moments we'll share in this series.

Acknowledgements

"For every leader in the challenge of working with their top leaders"

preciouseda@gmail.com

Preciouseda.blogspot.com

+2347086668850

Introduction

On vision

This issue, I must say, is one of, if not, the most notoriously taught topics. There's hardly any motivational speaker or life coach or teacher that hasn't talked about vision. This tells you that the topic is terribly important to leadership and to personal development. For any issue that keeps repeating itself severally in several places by several people, that issue is one that touches on life. I think vision is one issue that really deals with living or if I should be more precise, it is a matter of life and death.

Now, let's check this out, if you dropped off at a bus station and got into one of the buses and sat down, probably you had paid for the ticket before entering and when everyone was seated with the bus now full, suddenly a man leading a blind man walks towards the bus, and then before your eyes he leads the blind man to the driver's seat and hands him the keys to the bus. What would be your reaction? Well, I'm sure you're thinking what I'm thinking. So you see why I think it's a matter of life and death. Life depends on vision. The wise King Solomon wrote in his

Proverbs that people perish for lack of vision. Life is nothing without vision.

The connection between vision and living is something I've tried to discuss in simple terms. How our lives can be vibrant or dormant due to the presence or absence of vision is part of what this book deals with. When I refer to vision here, I must say at this point, it's not the vision achieved with the physical eyes I mean. Yeah, though I used the example of a blind driver at the beginning, it's just an illustration to demonstrate how important vision is to people. Like I said early on, every single leader understands to some extent what vision means and how it is important to leadership. But the reality remains that only a few leaders exploit the power in waving the wand of vision effectively.

Many times when we read and study on this issue, we get all the points and insights, but we hardly make progress because we many times find it difficult to implement all we have learnt. How can we move from knowledge to experience? That is the key question in the hearts of many leaders.

If every leader experienced what they knew, undoubtedly, the world would be a much better place than it is today. In this book, we'll try to see how we can bring into reality all that exists in knowledge with quite simple and few steps.

You may argue that this issue is too complex to reduce to few steps and should need some in-depth analysis and continuous learning to master, I agree with you, but we already have analysed so much that there is hardly more to analyse. It is time to bring to life every dream and hope and aspiration for yourself and your leadership. So this work will help get that to work.

The importance of vision; how to get a vision, how to bring a vision to reality and stuff like that. These are the matters we will discuss in clear simple terms and at the end we will have some effective action points to work on. So I do hope you get to read on and try to apply the simple but effective strategies in this book to your life and your leadership.

First - What's with vision

The most powerful tool available for man in his efforts to live is the mind. For quite a long time I had thought that when people say ***"whatever the mind can conceive the hand can achieve"***, they were just trying to motivate others and really never meant what they said. But after a few things I've experienced as a leader, I have cleared every doubt I used to have over that statement and today I can tell you for sure that whatever the mind can conceive, the hands can achieve. Vision is a product of the mind machine. Environment, circumstances, people form component parts of the mind machine and then desire serves as fuel. When all these come into play, the mind conjures up a vision and this vision drives the individual to work towards bringing into reality what has been seen in the mind. It works in same way with a group or an organization. What the mind of the leaders of the organization can conjure, the group can pursue.

I will not try to give any straight jacket definition to what vision is, but I can tell you how important it is to our lives and the lives of our people.

Have you ever sat down to think of where you would like to be sometime later in your life? When you think of certain aspects of your life, do you have any preferable desires? If your answer is yes then you can clearly understand what vision is. Vision entails having a clear picture of what you want to be, where you want to go and how you're going to end up after some time. There is hardly anyone living on earth that doesn't have a vision.

Have you ever sat down to think of where you would like to be sometime later in your life? When you think of certain aspects of your life, do you have any preferable desires? If your answer is yes then you can clearly understand what vision is. Vision entails having a clear picture of what you want to be, where you want to go and how you're going to end up after some time.

There is hardly anyone living on earth that doesn't have a vision.

When you go to sleep each night, you hope to wake up the next morning and do something, even though many people do not have a clear plan for their next mornings, it shows we all have visions. We go to sleep with the hope of waking up the next day, that's vision. So yeah, vision is one cool thing we've all got, but I'll be more direct with the importance of having a vision individually and corporately. And as mentioned earlier, the vision here has to do with having a desired goal or state of affairs for your life and for your people.

Second - Why do we need vision

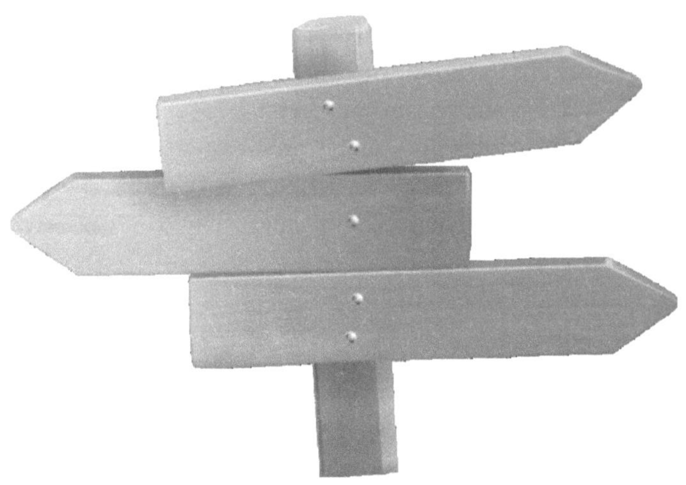

Vision makes life meaningful: If you could imagine your life without the ability to think, that would be a starting point to understanding what vision really means. If our minds could never arrange any thoughts or help us imagine anything at all, I can only imagine what kind of life we would have as humans. We would be no different from dulls or dummies. Our ability to imagine and think things in our mind makes our living more eventful. We plan the words we want to say and how we would say them, we think of the food we want to cook and how we would like it to taste, we see good clothes and good cars and just imagine if we had them. Our lives make more sense because we have the ability to think and produce vision. Life would be meaningless without vision.

Vision brings progress: Every invention or innovation the world has ever known and will ever know all started and will all start from the mind of the inventors or innovators. Humanity can be proud of the progress we have achieved throughout all the ages simply because people used their minds. It is impossible to create what you have never imagined.

To make something new happen, something new must first happen in your mind. We owe our civilization to the visions of great men and women who have been able to look beyond the surface of things and see things that were never thought of by ordinary everyday people. In our individual lives, our visions have brought us progress too; we dream of living comfortably and earning money, so we decide to make some progress by getting educated academically, we get a degree and apply for jobs, and then we get the job and begin to pay bills and afford what we had seen in our imagination, that's progress. It was propelled by vision.

Vision brings focus to living:I have seen quite a number of people who say things like *"all I want to do is just to be able to take care of my family"*. That's a clear target. Some people would tell you they just want to build their own houses, or buy their own cars, or just have a big wedding ceremony.

You would never dream up any of those without vision. Your whole life is driven by the desire to do that thing you think is the most important to you. For some other people, it's just to be able to afford the meal for the next day, or the rent for the next month. All the energy and time is invested towards achieving the one desire. That's focus, and vision brings that focus to the fore. Nothing explains this focus issue like students preparing for an important final examination. Everything that happens in the school environment is somehow arranged in view of the exam. The times spent on playing, sleeping and reading are all put into tailored specifications to enhance the ability to perform well in the exam. The eating habits are even changed to ensure the body and mind are in good shape for the exam. That's focus. When you have a vision for your life and your people, everything you do seems like a performer on a stage in a hall with twenty spotlights all shining on the one stage and on that one performer.

Vision brings speed to achievement: My most admired athlete is Usain Bolt. I recall watching him break the world record in the 100 meters sprint at the 2012 Olympics in London. By the time he had crossed half of the track his eyes were not looking over his shoulders to see who was hot on his heels. Bolt could be seen looking at the clock and trying to beat the time. At the end of the race, he had broken his own record. I thought to myself much later on, "this is what vision can do…it gives you speed". Many times we never get to where we want to be in good time and as planned because we shift away from our visions or we have no clear visions at all. You see, in that race at the Olympics, I'm quite sure most of the other runners had come to run because they wanted to beat Bolt because he was the clear favourite to win, but Bolt had come to beat the time, he wanted to break his record. And so it didn't matter who was running with him, his first competition was the clock. His vision was to break the record.

This vision increased his speed; it pushed him to go faster than he would have gone if he had placed his attention on just beating the other athletes. When you have a clear vision and you keep working towards bringing it to reality, you grow faster in different areas relevant to making your dream come true. Like in the race with Bolt, while others came in to beat the champ, the champ came in to beat the time. And so while others struggled to get the silver and bronze medals, Bolt was already assured of the gold medal, he was actually fighting for an extra medal; the world record.

Vision brings difference: The difference between what happens to you tomorrow and what happens to the other person tomorrow comes down to what you both see in tomorrow. Because we all have different visions, we achieve differently. Even though we all have similar desires of success and having a good life, we will never end up in the same place because we never see exactly the same places in our visions. Vision brings difference.

If you find ten people who want to buy a new car and ask them what they want, they would all tell you they want new cars, but there would be differences in the kind of cars they all want. It would be strange if they all tell you they want the same cars. Even if their cars may all be made by the same company, they would not be the same models. It is because vision is person specific. It is almost as unique as our DNA's. As our finger-prints are different, so are our visions for life different. That's why you can never reach real success running on another person's vision for life. You should have your own plan and goal for your life if you want to be different. One of the problems we have in the leadership of our world today is the fact that many leaders are leading their people with the visions of other leaders. There is nothing wrong with copying good styles of leadership and following the success stories of other great men who have gone before, but the mark of an effective leader is the ability to learn from others while forging your own path by giving due consideration to your uniqueness and the uniqueness of your own people.

Third - What can we take away from all that

The importance of vision can only be restated over and again, and we can never exhaust all the points that can be raised. But you really do not need to know all the points to become better, just know that vision is important. That's the starting point.

So what can we learn from all the above for ourselves and our people?

- If you haven't got a clear vision for your life and your people or group, you might just be living a meaningless life and your group may just be existing without any essence. Get a vision.

- We all desire to move forward and make good progress with our lives and the people we lead; our families, friends, colleagues and all those people we have some influence over. We cannot grow in all areas of our lives and with the people we affect without our having a clear vision for us and for them. Get a vision.

- Sometimes or most times life feels like there are so many things we would love to do, so many places we would like to go, and so many people we really want to be with. The reality is we can never be at all the places we want at the time we wish, we can never be with all the people we love to be with and we can never do all we want to do at the time we want. Vision will help us see the true desires we have and help us prioritise. Vision will help us focus on the most important things and ensure we get to do especially those things that can guarantee our happiness in life. Get a vision.

- I read a book by Brian Tracy, he's a mentor. He wrote Goals: How to get what you want faster than you ever imagined. Guess what? In that book, one of the most important points Brian spent a lot of pages on was vision. We have lots of dreams to reach and things to achieve, but we almost always never get to reach all our desired heights of success. Having a clear vision can be the magic wand that changes everything and gets us there faster than we ever thought we could get there. Get a vision.

•

Our world is burdened with huge bags of waste tagged '*No Originality*''. We have everyone climbing the ladder to success in personal life and organizational existence with the same ropes. We are losing our fibre of authenticity as the days go by. Lack of clear outlined visions will make us all copycats. No other person has the kind of life you have, no one can see the things you were created to see. If we must be original with the life we live and the things we hope to achieve with our people, we have no option but to be different from every other person around us. Our personalized vision will strike the mark that separates us from the rest of the world and make our leadership different regardless of all the striking similarities that abound in our world. Get a vision.

So with all we have said with how vision is important and what it really means to have vision and all the great things we could benefit from having vision, the next question we should consider is how can we get a vision?

Now this question is important because for many young leaders, when we read the materials and experiences of great leaders who have gone ahead of us in taking their people to great heights, we have the tendency to take in every information and apply them straight jacket to our lives and our people without really understanding that they are principles that require us to properly ascertain where they would be most beneficial before applying them. The stories of great men are cool, but we should apply their principles with good understanding and huge regard given to our peculiar lives and circumstances of our people. The point is, with getting a vision; it has to be person and people specific. Remember, vision helps create a difference between us and the rest of the world.

Fourth - How do we get our vision

*"Your vision will become clear only when you can look into your own heart. Who looks outside dreams, who looks inside awakens."*I think this quote from Carl Jung almost explains it all. How else can I make it simpler? Okay, the point is, you can only get a vision for your life and your people when you look at your life and your people. No sprinter runs and wins a race in the lane of another athlete. You are unique; you are not the same with the rest of the world. So no matter how beautiful and amazing the vision of another person is, it may never be suitable for your life.

You cannot spend another person's money on all you want and expect not to be in debt.

Your life and your people are markedly different from the rest of the world and so your vision and your people's purpose have to be customized to suit your uniqueness. So how can we get our customized visions?

- **Acknowledge that you are different:**One mistake we make many times is that we are very quick to draw all the similarities between us and many great people ahead. It is true that our lives may follow similar trends with those of successful people ahead of us, but we must learn to always remind ourselves that we are different in one way or another. Many times we are so quick to take crucial life decisions based on the inspiring similarities we see in our lives and the stories of others, but we must understand that yeah, principles can be universal, but circumstances are different. Circumstances may be the same but abilities vary. Abilities could be similar, but purpose is unique.

- **Know your difference:**The simple question that should flood your mind is, in what ways am I different? In your group, you should ask something similar; in what ways are we different? That's the starting point to acknowledging the good things within you.You cannot draw up a customized vision for your life and your people if you cannot tell the ways in which you are different from the rest of the world. Look at your values, your character, your biggest dreams and your deepest fears; these will light your path of thought in reaching your points of difference between you and the rest of the world. No matter how similar you may be with the people you admire the most, there are always points of differences. Just as our finger prints are markedly different, our DNA's are uniquely different, so are our life purposes. Finding that purpose highlights you in the crowd.

-

Acknowledge every good thing in you: For so many people, the only good things they know about their lives are the things they saw and have copied from others. There's nothing they've ever done by themselves, there's no idea they've ever gotten for themselves. It's funny but, for many folks, they really think it's impossible for them to do something different from what every other person is doing or has done.

Yes it's true that there's almost nothing new under the sun, but the hallmark of success is innovation and creativity. . The difference between Apple and Tecno is innovation, even though the two companies make mobile phones, their products are never the same because in many ways they have creatively marked out their uniqueness. So it is with our lives and our people, there are millions of leaders across the globe and there are billions of people trying to live life on earth, but the distinguishing factor between the numerous leaders lies in their ability to acknowledge the uniqueness within them. Everybody would be the same except some persons try to look inwards and awaken the specialty of their personality. I can assure you that if you really understood all that has been said, by now, like flashes of lightening, many things about your life would be flying through your mind.

You should be imagining those things you took for granted before now and how they are now important because they really show your true personality. By now you should be weighing all those decisions and choices you made that were influenced by the lives and decisions of others and you should be thinking of what you could do to make the difference. If your mind has ran through thoughts like that, then you should be ready for the next two points. For me, the next points are probably the most important when it comes to vision and success in personal life and leadership. Knowing the vision and what to do is very important, but leaving it at just knowing will take us nowhere. We would still remain the kind of people we were before knowing. We may just acquire a new title of "*knowledgeable ignorant*", because we can say how much we know and say how we know so much but we would have nothing to show the world for all we know.

Fifth - What's next after knowing the vision

Write it down

One of my favourite verses in the Bible is **Habakkuk 2:2.**It says ***"…Write the vision, and make it plain upon tables, that he may run that readeth it." – KJV.***

Just spare a moment in your thoughts and look at those words. It sums up every point we'll be trying to make. From that verse, we can clearly see three things that are the essentials for succeeding with vision as the driving force. The first is simply writing down the vision. We all have good memories, but like they say, the faintest pen is better than the longest memory. We may forget the things we say, but once we write them down, they stick with us. Most people cannot recall their childhood dreams because they were very young when they had those dreams. But if those dreams were written down, they would still have them and perhaps they would have still pursued them. The importance of writing down our visions is just simple; so we can always see them. Remember it's called a vision; we have to see it with our eyes.

We have to bring it out from our mind's eye and put it where the physical eyes can see it. For memory sake, we must write down our vision.

Just writing down the vision on some paper is not all, writing it where you can see it always is key. Sometimes when we read or hear people tell us to write our vision, we just get a piece of paper and put things down then throw the paper in some place where we never find it again. Well, that attitude shows either of two things; either we really didn't understand what it meant to write down our vision or the things we wrote down weren't important to us at all. If we really wanted to get something to happen in our lives and for our people, and we got a clear vision, I'm pretty sure that even without anyone telling us, we would write down the vision on some good paper or in a good book where we can at least make reference to it and help remind ourselves of it.

Writing the vision down is necessary for ease of reference, for refreshing our memory, and for easy communication with our people. One of my biggest inspirations, *Somina Johnbull*taught me how to look at my vision every day and say it to my hearing. The point about vision helping you reach success faster comes into play at this instance. Because the vision is written where you can easily see it and read it, you remind yourself of it constantly, and by reading it to yourself always, you attract it.

The law of attraction states that what you focus on, you attract, and what you attract is what you eventually become. You naturally gravitate towards your dominant thoughts. So we just have to put the vision on paper. Now, just writing down the vision isn't the end, remember, there are three things we could learn from the verse quoted above.

And so we've got the next point.

Make the vision plain

Of what use is a book to you if it is written in a language you do not understand? A vision may be meaningless if it is too ambiguous.

Making a vision plane implies several things.

Firstly, a vision should be made easily communicable and understandable for the visionary and the people. The vision could be explained with several pages of notes, but it should be easily read and easy to understand. At a glance, an average reader should have an idea of what you intend with your vision. If your vision demands that you always have to give explanations when someone reads or hears it, that vision is not plain. In this sense, the words used in coining your vision should be simple words, easily understandable by as many people as possible.

Secondly, the vision should be realistic. Brian Tracy gave an example of a man who said the vision for his life was to achieve world peace. I laughed out loud when I read that.

If that man was the Secretary General of the United Nations, perhaps his vision would be understandable, but for a man who had no plans of going into politics or becoming at least the President of a powerful nation, it becomes confusing as to how world peace could be achieved by this single man whom no one even knew his name. The vision must be something achievable within a time frame and based on your originality and peculiarity as a person or group of people, that's what it means to have a vision made plain.

Run with the vision

At the introduction, I pointed out that one of the setbacks of success and leadership is lack of requisite action to knowledge acquired. If you must see your vision come to reality, you must do something about it every day.

*Sam Adeyemi*noted that *"success is the daily achievement of set goals and targets"*. Many of us leaders see success as a destination, but no, it is a process. It is not when you have achieved the vision or made it a reality that you have succeeded; it is what you do always about the vision to make it real that makes you a success or a failure. You must plan your daily agenda around your vision. You cannot be hoping to travel to the east by taking a flight headed for the south. Your flight plan must follow the eastern map. Many of us have great visions and desires for our lives and our people, but what we do every day clearly shows that we are headed for a different destination. Working continually and taking actions consistently in consonance with your vision is what running with the vision really means. Our people will never reach the vision if they are not always reminded of it and if they do nothing about it always.

Every plan we make, every decision we take must be built around our vision and every of our actions must have a cautionary question attached to them; is this in line with our vision? This is what it means to run with the vision.

Sixth - Your vision and you

It's easy to read or hear principles and just take them, but as leaders, we must understand that many things about leadership, both at the personal and community level can never be mastered without true experience. By this I mean that to grow in effective leadership, you must actually come across situations that task your effectiveness. When you face those matters that demand you to apply your wealth of knowledge to your peculiar situations and you do so and cause positive changes around you and your people, then it can be clear that you have learnt something. No one can get a vision for you. People may guide you, lead you and teach you, but nobody can get your vision for you. At some point, they'll have to ask you "what do you want?" If the people who inspire you and lead you never ask this question, then they may just be impressing some aspect of their own visions on you. I always tell people when I speak, *if you fail to make choices for yourself, you will live by the choices of others.*

People should be able to see you when they hear or read your vision statement because your vision is a direct reflection of who you truly are. If you have been seeing someone act in a particular way or live a certain kind of life and then one day you asked the person of his plans for life, you would either have a confirmation of your first impressions, or you would be amazed at what they say or be disappointed at their answers. When people sound unsure of what they want with their lives, you get frustrated for them because maybe you had expected more. For many people, by just taking a thoughtful look at them, you can just tell they have no vision for their lives. This kind of people seem to be carried away by every wind that blows, every new idea sways them, any new trend catches their attention. They make the largest percentage of every crowd. They hardly or never ask why things happen the way they do and are easily influenced by others. So when you see them, they are almost never able to come up with independent opinions.

You will always become a problem to yourself and your community if you fall into that category. For many others, when you see them, there is a sense of direction to the things they do, they look more focused and have an air of seriousness to the things they do, never do they rush into things and more simply, they have some sense of purpose in them. You know they've got vision when you see them. And even though many of them may not be able to clearly tell you a vision statement, they're always able to explain their intentions for doing the things they do.

Seventh - Is the vision different from the mission

Ok, I had to bring up this question because while I was in Law School this question was raised when we discussed Professional Ethics and Skills, and after nearly an hour of going back and forth on the opinions of members of my class, the conclusion sounded something like "whether it's vision statement or mission statement, just make sure you have a clear plan…" It was a hilarious moment when I thought about it again later after the class, but it was something close to a heated argument during the lecture.

The dictionary helps define the two terms, that is vision and mission, and frankly, they mean almost the same thing. When I look at how different people see things and approach their personal and community or group leadership, I discover that for some people it's the word mission they emphasise while for others it's the vision they advance. But the both indicate having a clear purpose.

For me I see the mission as the ultimate goal, while the vision represents the state of things when the assignment is done or the goal is accomplished and even in the process of being reached.

I could explain this with an example from the military. When a team of soldiers is sent with a task to capture or eliminate key opponent personnel in the course of a war, their mission is the task of taking out those personnel while the vision is to win the war. So the result of completing the mission of eliminating the personnel is reaching the vision of being victorious in the war. Again, the mission may be winning a war with the vision of gaining territories. And as you dislodge your opponent from territories, your vision is being reached. So it really depends on what you want to achieve. But like my Law School folks said, just get a clear agenda for your life. Know your purpose and run with it. Get a vision.

Eighth - What's to be done after all's been said

Well what's left is to do, do and do. I was in a seminar organised by the John C. Maxwell leadership company and when it was time for questions a guy stood up and for about five minutes he gave a lecture on how he had read all of John Maxwell's books and knew all the principles by heart and how it was a great opportunity for him to attend the seminar. When the leader who facilitated the seminar got up to respond, he bluntly told the young man how foolish he had been and how it would have been better for him to have kept quiet. What was his problem? First, it was questions and answers session and not a period for comments, and then he just tried to show the world how much he knew but that was the wrong moment to do so. His intention could have been good, but he had made lots of people feel inferior and not as knowledgeable as he was. And really, if he had read all of John Maxwell's books and knew all the principles, he should have known that leaders listen hard and never rush to speak.

The moral of the story is: you may just think you know so much and you have learnt so much, but always remember, the evidence of knowing is in doing. The difference between the mediocre and the excellent is that the mediocre has known it all but the excellent does it all. And no matter how much you may think you know, you could never know enough. Keep learning and try to keep doing.

We could spend weeks and months talking about vision, this work can never be all that there is about vision; it's just too short. But the idea is to make it clear in simple terms and as short as possible, but not lacking in the key material that leaders need to understand the concept and how important it is. There are not so many things you should do suggested here, but just the most important things.

If we look inwards and get visions for our lives and our people, if we try to communicate our visions to ourselves and to our people constantly, and if we plan our daily, weekly, monthly and annual agendas just around our visions and ensure to follow through every day, it is impossible for our lives to remain the same. Remember, it's not how much you know that matters; it's how much you do with what you know that's important.

Cool quotes on vision!!

"Vision without action is a daydream. Action without vision is a nightmare"– Japanese proverb

'Where there is no vision the people perish"– Proverbs 29:18

"Vision without execution is hallucination"– Thomas Edison

"To the person who does not know where he wants to go, there is no favourable wind"– Seneca

"To accomplish great things, we must dream as well as act"– Antole France

"A possibility is a hint from God, one must follow it"– Soren Kierkegaard

"The very essence of leadership is that you have a vision. It's got to be a vision you articulate clearly and forcefully on every occasion. You can't blow an uncertain trumpet"– Theodore Hesburgh

"Determine that the thing can and shall be done and then we shall find a way"– Abraham Lincoln

"Dreams are extremely important. You can't do it unless you can imagine it"– George Lucas

"Cherish your vision and your dreams as they are the children of your soul, the blueprints of your ultimate achievements"– Napoleon Hill

"If one advances confidently in the direction of his dreams, and endeavours to live the life which he has imagined, he will meet with success unexpected in common hours"– Henry David Thoreau

"Keep your eyes on the stars and your feet on the ground"– Franklin D. Roosevelt

"The real voyage of discovery consists of not in seeking new landscapes but in having new eyes"– Marcel Proust

"The gift of fantasy has meant more to me than my talent for absorbing positive knowledge"– Albert Einstein